Passive Income
For Pastors

By #1 Best Selling Author
Kelly Cole

Copyright © 2014 Minister Kelly Cole

All rights reserved.

ISBN: 149521852X
ISBN-13: 978-1495218521

DEDICATION

This book is dedicated to every man of God serving the Kingdom

FREE BONUS
Passive Income For Pastors Audiobook

Be Sure And Download The Audio Version Of This Book FREE Here:
http://www.PublishingForPastors.com/FreeGift

INTRODUCTION

First I want to congratulate you for investing in this book. Here is what I can promise you, I can promise you that this book will open your eyes to the endless opportunities there are for you out there to produce passive income by simply using what God has already put in you.

This process I'm about to share with you "Passive income for Pastors" came to me after I was invited to share at a men's conference about the mountain of money. I sought the Lord on what to share and this process came into my spirit and the Lord said share with my men how they can use what I have already put in them to produce passive income for their families.

So I say to you read the whole book, and Take The Actions it instructs you to take and you will began to make passive income.

> *[18] But thou shalt remember the LORD thy God: for it is he that giveth thee power to get wealth, that he may establish his covenant which he sware unto thy fathers, as it is this day. (Deuteronomy 8:18 KJV)*

First thing I need you to do is write the title of your last 10 sermons below.

_____
_____
_____
_____
_____
_____
_____
_____
_____
_____

By the end of this book you will understand why I had you create this list.

Ok now that you have listed your last 10 sermons let's jump into the process!

STEP 1

RECORD YOUR MESSAGE

STEP 1 – RECORD YOUR MESSAGE

Record your sermons every Sunday, not just on audio, you need to record them on video.

Every time you speak have someone record it on video.

Wednesday night bible study, Sunday school and when you travel to other church to preach or teach.

After you have your message recorded make sure you edit it or have it edited for you. Add an intro and outro, be sure to include info of where viewers can reach you for more info about your ministry or products.

STEP 2

TURN THAT VIDEO INTO A DVD

STEP 2 - TURN THAT VIDEO INTO A DVD

To create the DVD you want to upload it to Kunaki.com

Kunaki.com will duplicate, print and ship your DVD anywhere in the world for only $1.75 per DVD plus shipping .

We are talking retail ready packaging, your DVD will look so good it will look like it came off a Wal-Mart shelf!

Example

DVD Income Streams

Sell your DVDs on Ebay! – Did you know you can list up-to 50 items a month for FREE on Ebay? You only pay anything if your product sells. To sign up for an Ebay account is free all you will need is a paypal account.

Amazon.com – Sell your DVD's on Amazon.com, Amazon has over 150 Million credit cards in there system all you have the ability to push one button and order your DVD. To sell on Amazon its $0.99 per sale + other selling fees. To signup go the bottom of Amazon's website and click "Sell On Amazon" and follow the sign up instructions.

Your Website – Sell your DVDs on your website! Don't have a website? The best place to get one is www.PrimeTime-Marketing.com

Events – Sell your DVDs at events you get invited to speak at. Remember they are only $1.75 fully packaged from Kunaki.com. The best part about Kunaki is you don't have to order a bunch at one time, there is no min. or max you can order.

Bonus Tip – Create a DVD of the month club were you get your members or supporters to sign up to receive a new DVD every month right to their door step for only $20 a month. Let's do the math, $20 month x 200 people = $4000 passive income stream!

All passive income, you don't have to touch a thing! Kunaki is going to print and ship your DVD for you, right to your customers!

STEP 3

TAKE AUDIO FROM DVD & CREATE CD

STEP 3 - TAKE AUDIO FROM DVD & CREATE CD

To create the CD just like the DVD you want to upload it to Kunaki.com

Kunaki.com will duplicate, print and ship your CD as well, to anywhere in the world for only $1.75 per CD plus shipping and handling.

We are talking retail ready packaging, your CD will look so good it will look like it came off a big retailer's shelf!

CD Income Streams

Sell your CDs on Ebay! – Did you know you can list up-to 50 items a month for FREE on Ebay? You only pay anything if your product sells. To sign up for an Ebay account is free all you will need is a paypal account.

Amazon.com – Sell your CD's on Amazon.com, Amazon has over 150 Million credit cards in there system all you have the ability to push one button and order your CD. To sell on Amazon its $0.99 per sale + other selling fees. To signup go the bottom of Amazon's website and click "Sell On Amazon" and follow the sign up instructions.

Your Website – Sell your CDs on your website! Don't have a website? The best place to get one is www.PrimeTime-Marketing.com

Events – Sell your CDs at events you get invited to speak at. Remember they are only $1.75 fully packaged from Kunaki.com. The best part about Kunaki is you don't have to order a bunch at one time, there is no min. or max you can order.

Bonus Tip – Create a CD of the month club were you get your members or supporters to sign up to receive a new CD every month right to their door step for only $20 a month. Let's do the math, $20 month x 200 people = $4000 passive income stream!

All passive income, you don't have to touch a thing! Kunaki is going to print and ship your CD for you, right to your customers!

STEP 4

CREATE MP3'S FROM THE CD

STEP 4 - CREATE MP3'S FROM THE CD

Ok now you want to take the audio from the CD and create Mp3's to digitally distribute them to all the online channel that will sell your mp3.

The easiest way I've found to do this is to upload your Mp3's to CDBaby.com and they will distribute it for you to the channel listed below.

There is a cost involved for CDBaby to distribute your mp3's, for a single mp3 the cost is $12.95, and for a whole album the cost is $49. To sign-up just go to CDBaby.com and click on artist sign-up and follow the instructions given.

MP3 Income Streams

Itunes

Google Play

Spotify

Amazon Mp3

Zune Store

Rhapsody

eMusic

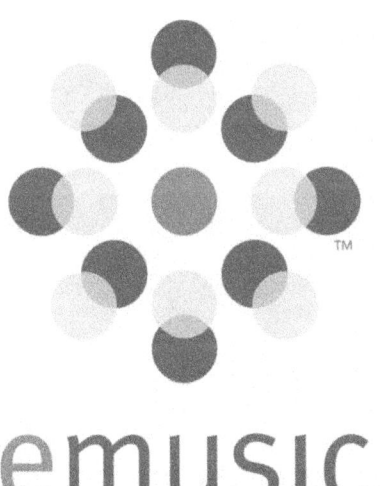

Your Website – Sell your MP3's on your website! Don't have a website? The best place to get one is www.PrimeTime-Marketing.com

Compiled List Of Mp3 Income Streams

- Itunes
- Google Play
- Spotify
- Amazon Mp3
- Zune Store
- Rhapsody
- eMusic
- Myspace
- Nokia
- Tradebit
- Myxer
- Your Website

Remember the best place to distribute your MP3's is CDBaby.com

STEP 5

**TRANSCRIBE AUDIO
& TURN IT INTO AN EBOOK**

STEP 5 - TRANSCRIBE AUDIO & TURN IT INTO AN EBOOK

Ok on this step you need to take the audio and type it out word for word or have somebody else do it then turn the written piece into an ebook and upload it to the ebook channels listed below.

To upload and ebook it will have to be formatted for the different ebook devices, you will also need a cover and more, **PrimeTime-Marketing.com** can handle all of the above for you including transcription services.

After you have all the pieces you can then upload your ebook to the following places.

Ebook Income Streams

Amazon Kindle – To upload to Amazon Kindle go to kdp.amazon.com and sign-up for a free account. After you sign-up just complete the step by step process to upload your ebook.

Below is a screen shot of kdp.amazon.com
Click Sign Up To Get Your Free Account

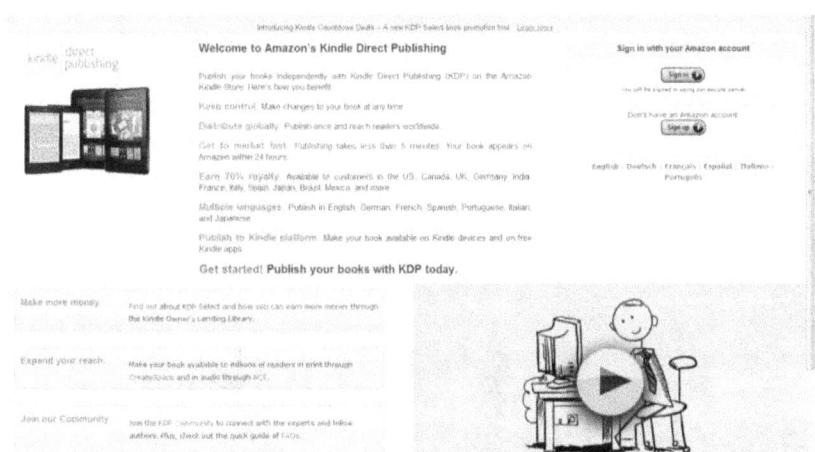

You will have to fill in form & Update Tax Info before you can upload an ebook.

To upload your ebook to the websites below there is a website called **Smashwords.com** that will distribute your ebook to all of them.

Nook

i-books

Kobo

Sony Ereader

STEP 6

TURN THE EBOOK INTO A BOOK

STEP 6 – TURN THE EBOOK INTO A BOOK

Now that you have your ebook done, it can also become a physical book.

Becoming a Published Author Will Open Up So Many Doors / Opportunities You Probably Never Dreamed Of!

If you have ever wanted to be invited to speak at a conference, workshop etc. A book puts you inline as the expert!

Think about not only will you get an honorarium for speaking, you can now go in the lobby & sell your books and put more spending cash in your pocket! Imagine that flight home with an extra $1,000 - $2,000 in your pocket!

All you will need to do is format your manuscript that was transcribed into the correct book size. The standard book formatting size is 6x9.

Book Income Streams

Amazon – The #1 book retailer on the internet, it is the place you want to be as a published author.

Books-A-Million.com

Barnes & Noble .com

Events /Speaking Engagements - Sell your Book at events you get invited to speak at.

BONUS TIPS

Create Training Videos with a program called Camtasia – Are you an expert at doing something? Like writing sermons, building a church or church fundraising? If so you can create a training course teaching your expertise. Simply record yourself teaching and apply the steps above. If it is something that you can teach on the computer use Camtasia which is a program that records everything you do on your computer and turns it into a video.

A great place to sell a training course is a website called **www.Udemy.com**, Udemy is a marketplace full of training courses and How to videos that range from and topic you could dream of.

Record Audio With Audacity – In step 3 we talked about removing the audio from your video and creating a CD. Well if you don't have a video recording and you would like to create audio products, you can download a free software call Audacity and record audio trainings & teachings. (Go to **audacity.sourceforge.net**)

Use Freeconferencing.com to do tele-seminars and conference calls that teach a topic. After the call they will send you an MP3 that you can then follow the steps in this book.

Create your own BlogTalkRadio.com show – Use Blog Talk Radio as a platform to interview amazing people and create products from the interview mp3. Interview Experts In Any Field!

Apply the steps in this book and Teach What You Know!

> 4 He becometh poor that dealeth with a slack hand: but the hand of the diligent maketh rich.
> Proverbs 10:4 (KJV)

STEP RECAP

Step 1 – Record Your Message On Video

Step 2 – Turn The Video Into A DVD

Step 3 - Take Audio From DVD & Create CD

Step 4 - Create MP3'S From The CD

Step 5 - Transcribe Audio & Turn It Into An Ebook

Step 6 - Turn The Ebook Into A Book

> **"BE STRONG AND OF GOOD COURAGE, AND DO IT..." 1 CHRONICLES 28:20**

PASSIVE INCOME BLUEPRINT

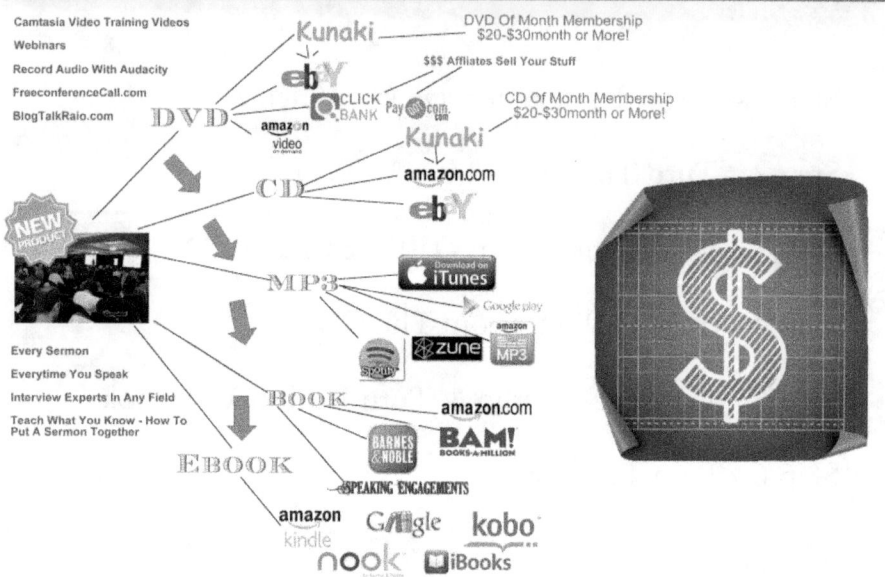

Total Income Streams

43 Total Income Streams from one Message!

If you just made $100 day = $3,000 month

$200 a day = $6,000 month

Passive Income $$$

Passive Income Empire

DVD
Video Course
CD
Mp3's
Ebooks
Paperback Book
From 1 Sermon Recorded On A Sunday!

Now referrer back to your list of sermons I had you write down in the beginning, now as you can see you either have the sections for your first passive income product or you have the titles to 10 different products.

If you don't do but one step in this process, you need to do step 6!

Every pastor should have a book!

Becoming a Published Author Will Open Up So Many Doors / Opportunities You Probably Never Dreamed Of!

If you have ever wanted to be invited to speak at a conference, workshop etc. A book puts you inline as the expert!

Think about not only will you get an honorarium for speaking, you can now go in the lobby & sell your books and put more spending cash in your pocket! Imagine that flight home with an extra $1,000 - $2,000 in your pocket!

I Know You Want More Money!

I Know You Want A Change In Your Life!

I Know You Want A Job That Every day Is Payday?

I'm Going to Sell You On Doing The Things You Know You Should Be Doing...

I'm Going to Sell You On Taking The Actions You Know You Need To Take!

I'm Going to Sell You On A Whole New Life Of Freedom!

Take Out A Clean Sheet Of Paper And Write These Words

TAKE ACTION NOW!

Because Tomorrow Never Comes...
What You Don't Do Today, Doesn't Get Done!

What I'm About to share with you will change your life!

I'm Going to Share With You The Ultimate Publishing Package!

Before I Found My Passion…

I Worked Two Jobs 16-17hr Days To Support My Family!

I Used To…
- Be afraid to lose that job I hated..
- Have ask to go to my son's football & basketball games
- Can have a day off for my Anniversary, to take my wife to dinner
- Get in trouble if I took too long on break!

Not Anymore!

I thank God he has blessed me with opportunity to help people's dreams come true, to become published authors!

This young lady is Jessie Rogers, she is 16 and was born blind. We made here dream come true of becoming a published author.

WOW She is 16 & Born Blind and you still making excuses?

More People We Made Dream Come True

It was always a dream of mine to see a book on the shelf with my name and face on it.

Prime Time Marketing was easy to work with, and took care of everything and at a very reasonable rate!

Thanks again Kelly for everything you did to make another one of my lifetime dreams come true

Melanie Harris
Author of "On This Journey"

With writing my first book, Kelly Cole & Prime Time Marketing have exceeded my expectations.

Kelly's love for what he does pleasantly flowed into every aspect of the publishing process.

His drive and ability to go beyond expectations enforces my desire to work with him and Prime Time Marketing again soon.

Tawana R. Powell
Author of "Life Fulfilled"

When I Started My Business…
I got invited on a Tele-call….

The guy on the call told me exactly what to do to make my dreams come true.

I Told Him, He Was Crazy!

Guess What?

I didn't TAKE ACTION…And It Cost Me At least $50,000!

Yes I achieved some Success, but had I Took Action then on what he shared with me, my Success would have come a lot faster!

When I Started To Take Action!
I Started Making Money!

Write This Down

Successful People Don't Ask How Much Something Cost, They Ask How Much Will It Make Me!

Question?

How Do You Win At Monopoly?

YOU BUY EVERYTHING!

I Have A Book Publishing Package Called The Ultimate Publishing Package!

Retails For $1497
Completely Turnkey!

Here Is What It Includes!

We Will Publish your book on Amazon & Amazon Kindle, Barnes & Noble, Books-A-Million & More!

Book formatting & Editing

Unique ISBN #

Book Cover Design

Physical Copies Of Your Book

Complete Marketing Plan

Book Trailer / Promo Video

Your book will print & ship on-demand, you won't have to touch a thing!

Complete Passive Income!

Plus you will receive a link to order your book wholesale if you would like to have more physical copies to sell in person.

As low as $2.15 per book!

Plus you will maintain all rights to your work & 100% of your profits.

What If I Told You All You Had To Do Was Give Us Your Manuscript?

Your Ultimate Publishing Package
<u>**Sets Up Everything For You!**</u>

All You Have To Do Is, Give Us Your Manuscript!

The Ultimate Publishing Package

- We will Publish your book on Amazon & Amazon Kindle, Barnes & Noble, Books-A-Million & More!
- Book formatting & Editing
- Unique ISBN #
- Book Cover
- Plus Physical Copies Of Your Book
- Complete Marketing Plan
- Book Trailer / Promo Video
- Book will print & ship on-demand
- Order your book wholesale
- Maintain all rights to your work & 100% of your profits.

Your Ultimate Publishing Package
Sets Up Everything For You!

All You Have To Do Is, Give Us Your Manuscript!

The Ultimate Publishing Package
Retails For $1497

If All The Ultimate Publishing Package Did for you was put an Extra $2,000 in your Pocket from publishing your book…

How many of you would be almost certain it would be worth $1497?

You Going To Find Out That The Investment Is Way Better Than $1497!

You Can Do THIS!

It's In You!

Here Is What You Need To Do, You Need To Get Signed Up For The Ultimate Pushing Package!

And Get Your Book Published!

It's Your Time To Hold Your Book In Your Hand!

The First 3 To Get Signed Up Will Also Receive The Following **FAST ACTION** Bonus!

My Generator Success Pack!

The Ultimate Publishing Package

Retails For $1497

But You're Not Gonna Pay That!

~~$997~~

~~$797~~

Get Everything For

$697

Get Started Today For Half Down

$348.50

Wait There's More…

We're Going To Take Off Another

$50 For Buying This Book!

Get Started Today

For Only $297

The Ultimate Publishing Package

- We will Publish your book on Amazon & Amazon Kindle, Barnes & Noble, Books-A-Million & More!
- Book formatting & Editing
- Unique ISBN #
- Book Cover
- Plus Physical Copies Of Your Book
- Complete Marketing Plan
- Book Trailer / Promo Video
- Book will print & ship on-demand
- Order your book wholesale
- Maintain all rights to your work & 100% of your profits.

Your Ultimate Publishing Package
Sets Up Everything For You!

All You Have To Do Is, Give Us Your Manuscript!

Get Started Today
For Only $297

There Comes A Point in Your Life When You Know You Need to Take A New Action

There comes a Point when the thing You know you Need to do is Obvious…

Years From Now You Going to Look Back at this Moment, You going to say he gave me the Opportunity To Change my Life!

Take Action Now!
Get Signed Up Now Go To
www.publishingforpastors.com/yes

Get Started Today

For Only $297

Get Signed Up Now Go To www.publishingforpastors.com/yes

ABOUT THE AUTHOR

Kelly Cole is the CEO of Prime Time Marketing, He's also a Minister, Speaker, #1 Best Selling Author, Consultant. He speaks and consults on internet marketing, starting an internet business, self-publishing your own book, social media & product creation.

Kelly Cole has authored and published over 15+ paperback, audio and e-books including

Conversations With Sharks -Success Secrets Shared By The Sharks On ABC's Hit TV Show Shark Tank **www.ConversationsWithSharks.com**

It's In You ~ How To Use Your God Given Gift To Produce Income Online

The 30day Take Over~ How To Takeover The Internet With Your Product Brand Or Service **www.30daytakeover.com**

Website Flipping 101 (**www.WebsiteFlipping101.net**)& Website Flipping 202 Video Course (**www.WebsiteFlipping202.com**) ~ How To Build & Sell Virtual Real Estate

"18 Ways To Create Info Product" Audio Course(**www.thegeneratorclub.com/productcreation**)

As an Entrepreneur & Internet Marketing expert and panelist Kelly has spoken and appeared in numerous conferences, workshops, seminars, radio shows and publications.

As an Consultant Kelly has worked with clients who have appeared on **OWN, Real House Wives of ATL, Bravo, NBA, WORD network, MTV, BET, Atlantic Records, and more.**

Prime Time Marketing Services

To Invest In One Of The Services Below Simply email us: info@primetime-marketing.com

Websites – start at $299 & Up (must request a quote based on needs)

Logo Design – $60

Complete Business Pack (Logo, Letterhead, Business Card Design & Brochure) – $497

8×10 Flyer Design – $60

4×6 Flyer / Postcard Design – $60

Business Card Design – $50

Brochure Design & Layout – $65

Press Releases $20

YouTube Promo Videos – $50

Online Lead Generation Package – start at $299 (A System to generate leads for your business)

Internet Marketing Campaigns – start at $197 & up

SEO Online Marketing – Start at $197 & Up (Based on Needs)

Custom Twitter Page $97

200-500 Twitter Followers $27

Custom Facebook Fan Page $97

200-500 Facebook Fans $27

Product Creation Consulting – By quote only based on needs

Book Publishing – Contact Us
(Comes with book on Amazon, Website, Book Cover, ISBN & More)

Book Covers – $47

Amazon Kindle Conversion / Publishing – $97

Book Ghostwriting Service – starting at $997

Celebrity Endorments – By quote only based on needs

T-Shirt Designs – $50

PRIMETIME MARKETING.
GENERATING IDEAS & MAKING DREAMS COME TRUE

If You Don't See Something You Need Contact Us – I'm Sure We Can Do It!

www.ConversationsWithSharks.com
www.PrimeTime-Marketing.com

HELPFUL RESOURCES

Prime Time Marketing http://primetime-marketing.com - Book Publishing, Web-Design, Logos, Flyers, Consulting, & More!

The Solution Coach – http://iamthesolutioncoach.com - Solution Coaching, Consulting and Strategy Sessions

Audacity http://audacity.sourceforge.net - Free software for recording audio

Amazon Kindle Signup Page – http://kdp.amazon.com

Udemy http://www.udemy.com – Place to upload and sell your training courses

Camtasia http://www.techsmith.com/camtasia.html - Record training courses by recording what's on your screen

Camstudio - http://camstudio.org – FREE Version of Camtasia, Record training courses by recording what's on your screen

FreeConfericing http://www.freeconferencing.com – Get a Free Conference call line record interviews and calls, receive a free mp3 emailed to you after the call

OpenOffice http://www.openoffice.org – Just like MS Office but Free! Write documents, do Powerpoint Presentations and more.

Any Video Converter http://www.any-video-converter.com/products/for_video_free/ - FREE Video Converter, Convert all videos & YouTube to MP4, MP3, etc. for various media players

VoiceBase http://www.voicebase.com – Free audio transcribing software, the clearer the audio the better the transcription

BlogTalkRadio - http://www.blogtalkradio.com Create your own podcast in seconds. No fancy equipment or software downloads needed - just a computer and your unique perspective.

Elance http://elance.com – Post any job you have that you need done, worker will bid on your project and you choose the one you like.

Clickbank http://clickbank.com – A marketplace for selling your digital training courses. It also thousands of people ready to promote your product for a commission.

MailChimp http://mailchimp.com - FREE place to design and send email marketing campaigns.

Pixlr http://pixlr.com – Free version of Adobe Photoshop, edit photos and create book covers etc.

My Ebook Maker http://www.myebookmaker.com – A site that lets you Create and format ebooks that are ready to upload to Amazon Kindle & more!

Spreadshirt – http://spreadshirt.com Open up a Free T-Shirt Line

Smashwords - http://www.smashwords.com Distribution for your ebooks to itunes, nook & more!

Marketing Resources

EzineArticle - www.ezinearticles.com Upload Articles for Free Traffic

PRWeb.com http://prweb.com Create and upload Press Releases

Turn Article Into A PowerPoint Presentation & Upload To Document Sharing Sites

www.scribd.com - DocStoc www.docstoc.com - SlideShare www.slideshare.com

Top Places to Upload Video

www.youtube.com - www.metacafe.com - www.dailymotion.com - www.vimeo.com

Squidoo www.squidoo.com – Create pages to promote your books, ebooks and events

If You Have Any Questions Email – info@primetime-marketing.com

Christian Hip Hop Artist Aaron Cole, Darren Higgins Jr. (D-Higgz) and Ben Goulds (R.A.Y.) have joined forces to form a super group called the Future Kings. All three young men agree it was a call from the Lord for them to come together as a group. The three young men along with young comedian Zack Dukes just completed a 14 city tour called The Future Kings Tour which they traveled to cities like Atlanta, Chicago, Memphis, Jackson & York, PA and more. It was while on tour that the Lord began to work on them individually about coming together as a group.

"At first I was completely against it" says Aaron Cole. "Reason being I already had my new solo album ready to go, I had my songs written, the title of the album and the concept and I just didn't want to push it to the side." "I didn't come around till the end of the second leg of the tour when we left Pennsylvania and the presence of the Lord was so strong that I could not deny that this is what He was calling us to do."

"I was the first on board, says Ben; starting the tour we were all doing 3 separate sets and deep down I really didn't like that. I felt the most comfortable being on stage with my brothers. The thought first entered my mind as we were leaving Chattanooga, because of the short amount of time we had to perform we decided to just stay on stage and rock together. That feeling of all three of us on stage at the same time was powerful; from then on I was sold out to the idea of us becoming a group."

"For me it took a minute to hear the Lord that we needed to be a group says D-Higgz" I like Aaron was focused on taking my solo career to the next level after the tour, but the more we performed together on stage the Lord begin to reveal to me that the group is where the blessing is."

The Future Kings plan to release their debut album in the fall of 2013. They are currently writing and browsing through beats from different producers. They are also planning a Fundraiser Concert and a Tour DVD screening to Raise Funds for the recording, packaging and marketing of the Album. Stay tuned and keep your eyes glued to what the Lord is doing with the Future Kings. Be sure and follow them on Twitter @FutureKingsTour, Like them on Facebook @FutureKingsTour and Visit their website www.FutureKingsTour.com

The Future Kings are also still taking dates to minister at events around the country. BOOK The Future Kings Tour For Your Next Youth Event! Email: futurekingstour@gmail.com or Call 276-229-0530

Quote Of The Day

"Don't Let What You Don't Have, Stop You From Using What You Do Have"

- Kelly Cole

www.ConversationsWithSharks.com

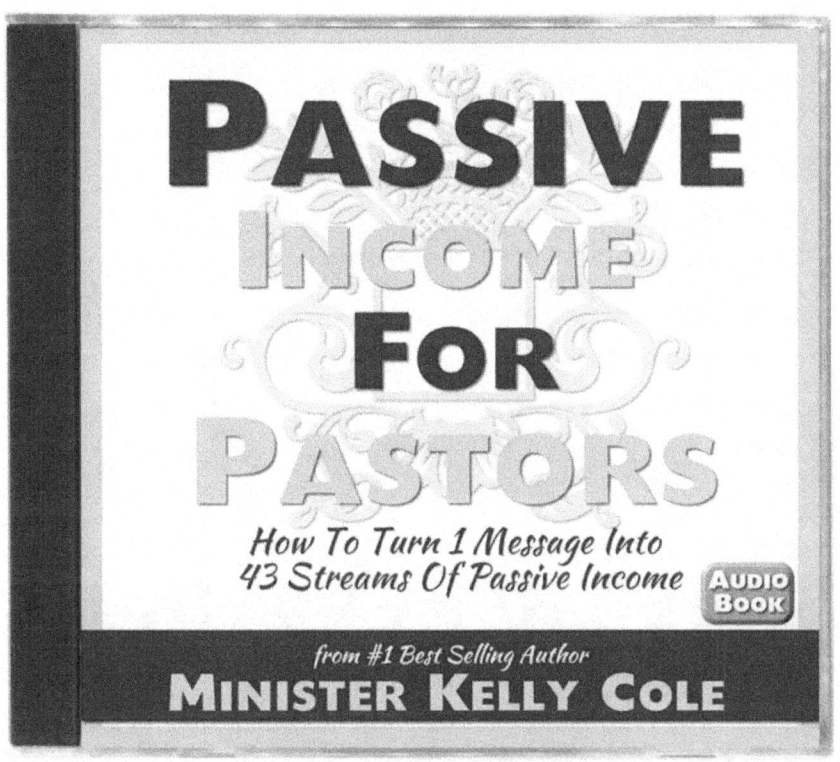

FREE BONUS
Passive Income For Pastors Audiobook

Be Sure And Download The Audio Version Of This Book FREE Here:
www.PublishingForPastors.com/FreeGift

www.ingramcontent.com/pod-product-compliance
Lightning Source LLC
Chambersburg PA
CBHW051820170526
45167CB00005B/2088